The Virtues of Internet Marketing

The Virtues of Internet Marketing

Chapter 1: The Art of Selling

Imagine a row of cramped stalls on the dusty road somewhere in the Middle East, several hundred years ago. The stalls sit side-by-side on both sides of a dusty street. Some people in the crowd are simply going from one place to another, and some have come to purchase a particular item. The vendors use all sorts of schemes and strategies to get the attention of the passersby and draw them to their own stall rather than to their neighbor's. Each vendor must convince one person at a time that he has the best product compared to all those around him and that it would be a grave mistake to buy from anyone else besides him. The buyer has to be convinced that what he is giving up is nothing in exchange for the value that he is getting in return.

The buyer has to be convinced that what he is giving up is nothing in exchange for the value that he is getting in return.

This is the art of selling.

Every business person, whether on a dusty street in the Middle East or in an air-conditioned high-rise in New York City, has to convince the buyer that his product is the best and that the buyer would be missing out on a great deal by walking away from the transaction. The object of the person or company selling the goods and services is to convince the buyer that he will get more than he is being asked to give.

People have been mastering the art of selling products and services to those who need them since the beginning of time. The methods

Contents

Chapter 1: The Art of Selling 4

Chapter 2: Show Customers the Value 8

Chapter 3: Be Authentic, Responsive, and Real 12

Chapter 4: Lead; Don't Sell 15

Chapter 5: Take Advantage of Social Networking 18

Chapter 6: Establish a Long-Term Relationship Through E-mail Marketing 20

Chapter 7: Reassure Your Customers 23

Chapter 8: Take the Lead in Your Niche 25

Chapter 9: Be Honest 28

Chapter 10: Give It Away 30

Conclusion 32

that entrepreneurs use to sell their goods have changed down through the millennia, but the principles are still the same.

No business exists without a buyer.

No sale happens until a buyer is convinced that he will benefit by making the purchase. The buyer has to believe that what he is giving up in exchange is worth less than what he is getting. A person who walks into a fast food restaurant values the meal more than the few dollars that the meal will cost. If the buyer doesn't perceive that he is getting more than he's giving, there is no transaction.

Selling online is no different.

Granted, the method of selling online is relatively new in the history of commerce, and there are certain unique strengths and weaknesses related to online commerce that did not come into play just a few years ago. Selling online is still selling, and the principles have remained unchanged down through centuries of business transactions.

One of the biggest complaints about online sellers is that the vast majority of them seem to think only about closing the sale.

Because of the universal reach of the Internet, it's easy for some online sellers to feel they can hide because they're not looking the buyer eye-to-eye over a counter in a retail shop. Buyers likewise also feel less secure because they can't see the seller face-to-face, and they usually cannot visit the store in person and reassure themselves of the legitimacy of the business.

These unscrupulous online sellers really have no regard for the customer; they value only what the customer can do for them, which is adding dollars to their bank account. It is quite possible for an online seller to build an entire business model on one-time sales rather than building a list of satisfied clientele who come back for repeated purchases.

That's the danger awaiting online sellers – the bad reputation of a few.

Other online sellers – the kind you want to be – couldn't be more different. They really do want to do the right thing, and they're aware of the need to provide honest value to their customers. Their desire is to provide significant value to the buyer at a fair price, but they sometimes struggle to communicate that value. Their heart is in the right place, but they have difficulty reaching out and convincing the buyer that they're different than the other group.

No business can succeed without a seller convincing a buyer to pay.

Even if your heart is in the right place, you'll have to develop the art of convincing people that you have what they need if you want to succeed in your online business. People browsing the Internet today have the attention span of the Middle Eastern customers walking down a dusty street, scarcely glancing at the vendors who shout for their attention. Online sellers must hold the attention of potential buyers and convince them that the products they are selling really can help them

solve their problems and can do it better and cheaper than anyone else's product can. What you are selling simply must be better, and you must also believe that it is better and be able to communicate that.

Whatever your product or service, you must be able to convince the buyer that what he gives up in return is less than the value he's getting by making a purchase from your online store.

It's your job to create the need, or at least to magnify it, so that you're standing ready with your product or service just as soon as the buyer is convinced of his need.

Chapter 2: Show Customers the Value

A well-known quotation goes like this: "I don't mind buying; I just don't like being sold." That expression rings true for a lot of Internet buyers. They don't mind buying more, even high-ticket items, if they feel they are getting more value than they're giving up. Whether it's $5, $500, or $5000, there's a buyer at each one of those price points if you, the seller, can convince him that he will get at least double his money back from the purchase.

It's not the dollar amount per se; it's the amount of expected return.

It's not about selling cheap, low-ticket items but about remembering that buyers always want more than they're willing to give.

You have to show them very clearly the value of what you're offering. It's the classic distinction between features and benefits. Features are things that a product can do, but benefits are what those features can do for the buyer. You need to focus on the benefit to the buyer by showing exactly what the buyer will be able to get by purchasing your product.

Today's Internet shoppers are savvy and skeptical. They've seen all kinds of gimmicks and scams and may have lost money in the past. With such a high level of skepticism, Internet buyers today must understand clearly what the product can do for them before they are willing to pull out their credit card.

Focus on the benefit to the buyer by showing exactly what the buyer will be able to get by purchasing your product.

There must be a reasonable match between the values the product is offering and the price that customers are being asked to pay. If there's too much of a discrepancy between the two, buyers will be suspicious. They'll think either that you're trying to scam them if the price is too high, or that there must be a trick if the price is too low. You can't really blame them, because there are many Internet marketers who are employing all kinds of unethical strategies just to get the buyer to click on the Buy Now button.

But you've already decided that you're going to be different – that's good.

What can you do to help buyers understand the value in your product?

1. **Show the value.** This is the point we've been discussing. You must reiterate the benefits of your product so that the buyer comes to associate those benefits with your product. Use every platform available: affiliate ads, banner ads, pay-per-click click campaigns, even classified ads. Your goal is that your product becomes synonymous with the benefits that it offers the buyer. When the buyer thinks of a particular problem, you want him to think of your product as the only solution for that problem.

2. **Be unique.** The marketplace today is flooded with products competing with yours, many of which are almost indistinguishable. What can you do to make your product

stand out? You have to find something about your product which is new or unique. People are very interested in the latest thing. No one is interested in last year's model, whether it's a cell phone, a DVD player, or car. People don't want average products, and they don't want outdated products. They want the latest thing so they can show their friends and brag on the great deal they got. You need to be aware of this tendency and market toward it. If you think you should be subtle, don't. Be bold and direct. Make sure the buyer knows what you have to offer compared to all the other products which seem very similar.

3. **Offer a guarantee.** Yes, it's true that some scam artists will put a "Satisfaction Guaranteed" image on their website with no intention whatsoever of offering money back to dissatisfied customers, much less answering an e-mail from a disgruntled customer. We've already determined that you are committed to be a different kind of online marketer. Giving a money-back guarantee gives the buyer a sense of reassurance when shopping on your website. If you're hesitant to give a full money-back guarantee, consider a free trial version with an expiration date, or a basic model with an offer to upgrade later to a premium model if the buyer is satisfied. The main point is that the buyer has to be convinced that you stand behind your product.

4. **Be honest**. There's really not another way to say this. It's true that every salesperson is committed to magnifying the benefits of this product and minimizing weaknesses. No one is asking you to do anything different. You must believe in the value of your product and be able to communicate that value

to the buyer. There are so many fly-by-night websites that make all kinds of claims and then disappear after a short period of selling online. The classic golden rule is one of the best guidelines for this aspect of your business: treat others as you would want to be treated. And it's also good to remember that people communicate more openly on the Internet about the experiences they've had. You want to do all you can to protect your online reputation. The last thing you want is blog posts and forum comments with consistently critical comments about your product. That's death to an online business. Be honest, be proud of your product, and be truthful about what it can and can't do. You may lose some sales in the short term, but in the long run your business will be built on a more solid foundation.

Chapter 3: Be Authentic, Responsive, and Real

One of Henry Ford's famous quotes is, "People can buy the Model T in whatever color they want, as long as it's black." As any car dealer can tell you today, those days of consumers accepting what they are offered are long gone. Buyers are finicky, they want what they want, and they don't like being told what they can or can't purchase. The days of cranking out products without concern for the interests of the buyer will never return. Online buyers who are succeeding today offer a wide variety of choices or even customizable products.

Establishing a relationship first is a big advantage, both in closing the deal and in developing future business.

People want products made for them, and the more unique, the better.

Any successful salesperson knows that establishing a relationship first is a big advantage, both in closing the deal and in developing future business. In the same way, an online marketer must let his true personality come through. You simply cannot hide behind the pages of your website. Companies that are succeeding in selling online demonstrate a personal touch in a variety of ways.

Here are a just a few examples:

- Auto-responders allow companies to personalize e-mails, using the first name of a potential buyer and making the e-mail sound as if it were written just for that buyer.

- A money-back guarantee that is personally backed by the seller's name and even a photograph can be a very powerful tool for combating buyer's remorse. People want to know that they're dealing with a person, and that person stands behind the product.

- Blogs are one of the greatest tools for showing your personal side. Customers appreciate interacting with the seller, before and after the purchase, so that they know they can get help if they need it, and they won't be left out in the cold.

- Successful online retailers have 24/7 support systems for their clients. Many people who shop online are doing it from a different time zone than the seller, or late at night, long after brick-and-mortar businesses have closed their doors for the evening. Customers need to know that they can get support at any time.

- Interactive surveys, especially in conjunction with a free gift, provide a great way for companies to interact on the personal level with their customers. The survey results also provide valuable market research, so that companies can target their offerings to the ever-changing needs of the consumer.

- It's important that there are products in all price ranges, whether you are selling products or services. Sometimes a customer simply wants to test the quality of your product without committing to a higher priced item, and some customers just don't have a lot of money to spend at this time. By offering lower priced items, you can give them a taste for the product and for the way the company interacts with its customers. Many of these customers who entered at a low price point will upgrade and stay with the company long-term, and they're satisfied with the treatment they've been given.

The days of the black Model T are long gone. **Customization, personalization,** and **flexibility** are the name of the game.

You need to be real, visible, and accessible if you want to succeed online.

Chapter 4: Lead; Don't Sell

People instinctively want to buy from the seller who's best in class. Only in rare situations will consumers gravitate toward a company in second or third place. Granted, every company would like to think of itself as being in first place, but statistically and objectively, that's just not true. There is a reason why brand names dominate around the world, whether soft drinks, movies, music, clothing, etc. People are willing to pay a premium for the brand name, and that's simply because of perceived quality.

*Your goal as an online seller is not to sell per se but to build your business into the **market leader position.***

Quality is a given with market leaders.

Your goal as an online seller is not to sell per se but to build your business into the market leader position. You need to dominate your niche and develop your brand name so that it's recognized as a leader. When times get hard, as they are now, people gravitate toward leaders, not willing to risk their money for a product that may be of lesser quality, even if the price is better.

So have you established market dominance as a leader in your niche?

1. **You must be visible.** As we discussed above, you are your brand name. Your personal name recognition is essential for dominance in your niche. There are countless ways to do this, but one of the most important is to get your name out

there and visible on the Internet. You can do joint ventures with other marketers, perhaps even competitors in certain situations. There's no rule against print advertising, such as magazine or newspaper ads. The pay-per-click campaign, managed effectively, can be crucial in building your brand name recognition. Even if people don't click through on the link, they begin seeing your name over and over again on various sites they visit. One interesting way many online marketers don't think about is running an affiliate campaign. If you have affiliates who are compensated for selling your product, then they have every motivation to spread your name in as many places as they can. While you may give up some of your profits because you have to reimburse the affiliates, what normally happens if the affiliate marketing campaign is run correctly, is that your business gains momentum and begins to grow exponentially.

2. **Establish your authority.** You must be seen as the "go to" person in your niche. People automatically trust and take advice from authority figures. There are many ways to establish yourself in this position, and some of the more well-known methods are article writing, forum posting, and publishing e-books. Each of these methods will add to your authority as time goes by and more and more people become familiar with the quality of your work.

3. **Polish your blog.** Your blog is the one place that existing and potential customers can hear your real voice. Put your picture on your blog. Talk about your life. You are not obligated to reveal everything about yourself, but blogging gives your readers a taste of who you are as a person. Then, when you need to speak as an authority, they will be more

likely to accept what you say. Of course, we should point out that authority once again can be quickly lost due to careless writing or factual errors. Pause and think before you publish each and every post.

Think of people in your own life who are authority figures for you. Why do you view them as an authority? Most likely, it's a factor of knowledge, experience, wisdom, and that gut-level instinct of knowing what to do and what not to do. The same principles will hold true in Internet marketing; you simply use different tools to get to the same goal.

Building your authority takes time and effort.

While there are many companies that claim to have a shortcut to establishing your authority, there really is no better way than the old-fashioned way. You must become known for consistent, persistent, and trustworthy content of the highest quality that actually helps people.

Chapter 5: Take Advantage of Social Networking

Internet marketing is all about people. Social networking is a great way for people to stay in touch, and it is still the most popular tool for friends to connect with friends. The three top social networking sites are by now known to almost everyone online: establishing a relationship first is a big advantage, both in closing the deal and in developing future business.

Find the delicate balance between being a helpful resource and monetizing your social networking sites.

- Facebook (www.facebook.com)
- MySpace(www.myspace.com)
- Twitter (www.twitter.com)

In addition, more sites are coming online and growing in popularity every day.

It's important to remember why people use social networking sites.

It's to stay in touch with friends. You need to keep this in mind as you think about your Internet marketing strategy. If you have ever had a friend or family member who was involved in network marketing, then you are familiar with the challenges. Have you ever had to cut off all contact with certain "friends" because they simply could not stop talking about their "opportunity"? Their inability to turn off the business spiel may ultimately cost them the relationship. That's the last thing you want to happen to you in your social networking campaign. While it's true that people come to your site with the understanding that you are selling products, you need to

find the delicate balance between being a helpful resource and monetizing your social networking sites. This balance may differ depending on the type of business that you have. But the main thing to ask yourself is, "Would I enjoy visiting my site?" That's a hard question to answer. But you have to ask it.

It's important to remember the basics. People like to hang out with her friends. They like to buy, but not be sold. Keep these principles in mind as you develop your social networking strategy.

Chapter 6: Establish a Long-Term Relationship Through E-mail Marketing

From a cost perspective, e-mail marketing is a tremendous boost to the bottom line. In the recent past, companies had to pay for printing, paper, and postage to stay in touch with their customers. And don't be deceived: off-line mail-order is alive and well today, and there is a place for off-line marketing when developing the long-term strategy of your online business. But, specifically, e-mail marketing is very powerful when managed correctly. There's a reason that people ignore most of their e-mails: They get too much spam.

Think about what you like as a consumer, and try to step into your customer's shoes when crafting your e-mail campaign.

E-mails getting stuck in the spam folder is the death knell to an e-mail marketing campaign.

Also sending spam e-mails could be the death blow to your financial bottom line. With U.S. government laws increasing the penalty for Internet marketers who send unsolicited e-mails, the risk is just too great for your online business to neglect compliance with this new law. At minimum, you should use your auto responder tool to ensure that everyone receiving your e-mails has opted in voluntarily.

If you would like to research more about the penalties for Internet marketers who send unsolicited e-mails, go
to www.fcc.gov/guides/spam-unwanted-text-messages-and-email
for more information.

As far as e-mail marketing is concerned, you want to remember that the main idea is to build relationship with your customers for the long-term. Your goal is not to amass a list of hundreds of thousands of people who couldn't care less about your business. Your goal is to stay in touch with your client base and present the latest news about your products and services to customers who may be interested.

With those goals in mind, here are some tips on how to develop an effective e-mail marketing campaign:

1. **First impressions count.** Craft your first e-mail very carefully. Sign up to receive your own e-mails and look at your message as it comes into your own inbox. How does it look? If you were a disinterested customer, would you click on it? Because your first e-mail will follow closely after the customer opts in to your list, the odds that they will read it are high. However, you simply must grab their attention on this first e-mail and provide them with excellent content, or they'll probably never open another e-mail from you again.

2. **Make sure the quality of the content stays high.** People read e-mails in order to get information to learn things that will help them in their daily lives or businesses. They do not read e-mails to be sold. Be sure to provide good-quality content so people actually look forward to getting your e-mails. Use subheadings, bulleted lists, and short paragraphs to break up the content and make it more readable.

3. **Be careful not to raise the reader's expectations too high.** The plan is that you will be sending them lots of e-mails, so don't set a standard for yourself that you can't keep. It's better to under promise

and over deliver than to have one awesome e-mail followed by a string of mediocre ones.

4. **Try to add value with every e-mail, even if it means giving away something for free.** The free item doesn't have to cost you anything. It could be something that you've learned from your experience, like a great website, the free report, a coupon for future purchases. Remember that anything associated with you and your business, even if it's free, has to be of the highest value.

5. **Entice people to interact with you in the body of the e-mail.** Use hyperlinks and HTML buttons to encourage people to click through to your website.

6. **Spend extra time on the title of the e-mail.** Be aware of the appearance of the e-mail on the various tools that people use to browse the Internet, such as smart phones and other handheld devices. Your title must grab their attention within the first few words. Make sure that you communicate in the title of the e-mail why they absolutely must open your e-mail and read your message.

Think of e-mails that you enjoy getting. Do you look forward to getting e-mails from a particular business? If so, why? Are there lessons you can apply from that business to your own? Think about what you like as a consumer, and try to step into your customer's shoes when crafting your e-mail campaign.

Your goal is that your customers look forward to getting your next e-mail and open it the first time.

It's all about the long-term relationship.

Chapter 7: Reassure Your Customers

Consumers are naturally apprehensive after purchasing a product. They fear that they've spent money in vain, spent too much money, or acted impulsively. Your job is to eliminate this buyer's remorse as quickly and thoroughly as possible. Depending on the type of product or service you're selling, it's most likely that people will have some questions about it. If it's software, they'll have trouble installing it. If it's an e-book, they'll have questions about certain sections. Whatever product or service you have, people have questions about it. You need to be there for them during this initial questioning in order to build trust and have a chance at future sales.

Your job is to eliminate buyer's remorse as quickly and thoroughly as possible.

There's nothing more frustrating than a web company that disappears after the sale.

If you have software to manage your help desk, make sure it works at all times and that customers get quick responses to the questions. A good idea is to send an automatic message as soon as the person has submitted a request, confirming that the request has been received and will be addressed promptly.

If your product is a bit complicated, you may want to offer a video tutorial explaining how to use it. This could be on your thank you page after the payment is processed. On the same download page, you should include full contact information for how to reach your company in case there are questions or concerns. This is the one time in which you want to make yourself the most accessible, because your client has just purchased a product from you and doesn't know you that well. You need to establish that you are fully committed to providing support after the sale.

If you're selling physical products, you could slip in a CD or DVD at practically no additional cost. Another idea is to send a follow-up e-mail, or even a phone call, after a few days to make sure that the person has not experienced any problems with the product. This follow-up will earn you respect and admiration and in almost all cases will lead to a long-term relationship with your new customer.

Chapter 8: Take the Lead in Your Niche

The Internet is a crowded place, and competition is intense. Visitors to your website owe you nothing because of the time you spent building your business. The best you can hope to get is a few seconds of their attention before they move on to the next site.

During those few seconds, you must quickly demonstrate how you are better than the competition.

Despite many examples to the contrary, the best way to grab the reader's attention is not by using flashing arrows or gaudy graphics. The kind of customer you'll attract by being glitzy will not stick with you in the long run; it's only a matter of time before someone else will come along with a flashier website. The way to gain a lasting edge over your competition is by providing quality information and taking care of your customers.

The way to gain a lasting edge over your competition is by providing quality information and taking care of your customers.

Here are a few ideas to help you think about your website and how you can pull away from the pack and take the lead:

1. **You must demonstrate at all times that you deserve to be the top website in your niche.** There should be no debate in the market that you are the best at what you do. At no point can you let customers' expectations fall short. Spread the word in as many places online because you can answer questions on blogs and forums, and always respond to

queries from customers. This process may take time, but you'll find yourself just a cut above the competition, and that's where you need to be.

2. **Have a clear pricing strategy.** Simply putting a $47 price tag on an e-book doesn't mean that it's worth that price, and you can slowly drive yourself out of business by undercutting your competition and offering a cheaper price than anyone else. Your goal is a fair price for fair product. You want customers who downloaded your products or purchased your services to be satisfied with the value they got for the price they paid. If your price is below your competition's, then there should be a good business reason to do so. If your prices are higher than your competitions, then you must provide additional value. It's all about delivering on your promises.

3. **Keep in mind your website is not a passive, unchanging cash machine.** You need to bring out new versions of your products continually, and keep seeking better ways to improve. Experiment with split testing, run time-definite promotions, and offer free samples to test market demand, etc., to thinking about new ways to promote your products and manage your business. Internet marketing is continually evolving, and so must your business.

4. **Remember that it's more expensive to get a customer than to keep one.** Never underestimate the value of a *returning customer*. Take good care of everyone who's purchased your products or services. Be attentive to customer complaints, and be quick to resolve queries and concerns. Remember that your customers don't know you; they don't know what a great person you are. You have to

prove it by your responsiveness to their needs. You must always honor your money-back guarantees just as you said you would: without hassle, without question, without delay. Your goal is to answer all support tickets, whether based on customer service or technical difficulties, within 24 hours. You'd expect no less yourself, if you were the customer.

5. **Be in touch with what your customers want.** Check out blogs and forums and other websites to see what people are asking for. It's not that you push your favorite products on them. Rather, you focus on what they want and provided to them. Don't be afraid to your unborn from time to time. If you've done something great to enhance a product, dubbed referred to say so. Customers are watching, and when they see that you have incorporated one of their suggestions into your next product, you'll gain the respect and their ongoing business.

6. **Know your competition.** This is true for any business, whether you are selling doughnuts, dry cleaning, or computers. At no point can you be caught by surprise. Sign up for your competitors' newsletters, watch their marketing strategies, and see whether there are strategies that you can implement. Be aware of what is going on around you so you can gauge your responsiveness to customers' needs and whether you need to move in a certain direction.

Chapter 9: Be Honest

The best salesmen and saleswomen down through the ages have told the truth. However, there's nothing at all wrong with an element of spin; to sell a product, you must stress the benefits. The selling is all about ethics and honesty. The old days of consumers accepting whatever they get from the company is giving way to online reviews on third-party websites, where consumers hold companies to account and are quick to point out product failings and shortcomings.

Consumers expect to pay a fair price for a fair product.

You do not want to be on the wrong end of those reviews.

You want customers praising your products, and to do that you have to be truthful about what you will and won't do.

Customers expect you to sell to them.

They expect to pay a fair price for a fair product, so they don't mind coming into the transaction with the understanding that your business exists to sell products. There are selling strategies that follow the in the realm of ethical selling. Consumers expect to see them, and it's not a violation of integrity to try to sell as best you can. A good example is what's commonly called up-selling. If you were asked "Would you like fries with that?" at a fast food restaurant, that is a simple example of up-selling. If a customer buys a product and somewhere during the selling process you offer another product that is slightly more expensive but has more benefits, there's no ethical issue in reminding a customer of another product that you have that might meet his need better, even if the cost is higher. If you believe that your product actually does solve customer problems, then there's no violation of your conscience to offer another product that you have in addition to the one that the person has just bought.

In a similar way it's perfectly ethical to down-sell, or offer a customer a great deal if they've declined your first offer. Suppose that the person is interested in your products, but is not interested in spending the money. Is there another product you could offer that would meet their needs but cost less? There's no problem at all in offering a lesser priced product if price indeed was the issue. You're simply offering another option that the person may or may not accept.

Always think of yourself and how you react when you're purchasing things online.

If you would like to click away from an offer how many pop-up boxes will you tolerate before you become frustrated? Internet marketers have all sorts of different opinions, but most ethical Internet marketers would agree that one or two pop-up boxes is acceptable, but past that point there is an increasing possibility of frustration as the person visiting your website is trying to exit but is continually blocked from doing so. Imagine yourself in a retail setting in which you decided not to buy anything that day. Can you imagine if the salesman blocked your access to the door? How would you feel about the owner of the store? That's exactly the feeling you do not want to have in the mind of your potential customer.

If someone would like to click away from your offer, then you have to allow it. If you block the door, you may lose a customer for life.

Chapter 10: Give It Away

Sometimes the best way to get a lifetime customer is by giving away something for free.

Remember that the free item must be something of value.

Everything you associate with your business, whether through a partnership with another marketer or a free item on your website, must be of the highest quality. Customers will know instantly whether you send them "free" report that is basically worthless, and that's the opinion they'll have of your company.

Everything you associate with your business must be of the highest quality.

Be equally careful about the quality of your **partners.** If you decide to run a *joint venture* with other Internet marketers, one of the best ways to do this is by having a giveaway event during which each marketer offers something for free in exchange for traffic to his website.

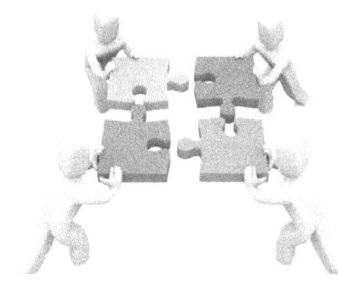

Remember that people come to the Internet for information, so a good way to build your business is by offering valuable content in an **e-course** that provides several messages over a period of time, such as a week or month. Free courses centered on a series of auto-responder messages are a great way to build a list, but you must make sure – as always – to deliver on your potential customers expectations. The content must be of high quality. Customers will expect that you will offer information about products that you have to sell, but you must be careful not to bombard them with sales messages. They signed up for content, and to keep up your side of the bargain, you must give them the content they requested. It's all about building your reputation as an Internet marketer of integrity, and anything you can do to increase their exposure to you will most likely secure their loyalty for a long time into the future.

In addition to free reports and e-courses, there are lots of things you can give away: podcasts, webinars, video seminars, website critiques, free samples of physical products, etc. You're limited only by your imagination; as long as you make sure that the giveaway item complements your business and provides actual value to your potential customer.

Conclusion

Internet marketing has changed the rules in many ways, but the principles of selling have not changed down through the centuries. Just remember to be yourself, hold to the highest standards of ethics, and integrity, and do for others what you would like them to do for you. If this is the model by which you run your business, you'll be well on your way to establishing a successful, thriving in business for many years to come

www.ingramcontent.com/pod-product-compliance
Lightning Source LLC
LaVergne TN
LVHW020454080526
838202LV00055B/5442